P9-AFI-264

DATE DUE

			PRINTED IN U.S.A.

The Jerusalem Windows

MARC CHAGALL

THE
JERUSALEM
WINDOWS

TEXT AND NOTES BY
JEAN LEYMARIE

GEORGE BRAZILLER   NEW YORK

Translated from the French by Elaine Desautels

First Revised Edition 1967

Second Edition 1975

Library of Congress Catalog Card Number 62–18146

*This edition of The Jerusalem Windows was printed and bound in
The Netherlands by Smeets Offset, Weert.*

TABLE OF CONTENTS

Page

INTRODUCTION vii

DIMENSIONS OF THE PREPARATORY DRAWINGS,
   THE STAINED-GLASS WINDOWS xix

TRIBE OF REUBEN 1

TRIBE OF SIMEON 9

TRIBE OF LEVI 17

TRIBE OF JUDAH 25

TRIBE OF ZEBULUN 33

TRIBE OF ISSACHAR 41

TRIBE OF DAN 49

TRIBE OF GAD 57

TRIBE OF ASHER 65

TRIBE OF NAPHTALI 73

TRIBE OF JOSEPH 81

TRIBE OF BENJAMIN 89

INTRODUCTION

Great works of art defy limitations of time and place, but sometimes strange combinations are required to produce such art. This is true of the Jerusalem Windows. They seem to belong to the distant past but were actually conceived in our own atomic age. Chagall's magic has made this unusual temporal paradox possible, and Zion, where stained glass was unknown, at long last has received the well-deserved mystic raiment for which it has waited since time immemorial.

It happened this way. In June of 1959, Dr. Miriam Freund, the National President of Hadassah, and Joseph Neufeld, the architect who designed the Hadassah-Hebrew University Medical Center, stopped in Paris on their return from Jerusalem and went to see Marc Chagall. At this meeting it was decided that Chagall would design the stained-glass windows for the synagogue that was to be part of the Medical Center.

Neither the choice of artist nor the time could have been more propitious. Like the great masters of the past, Chagall has always loved commissions that inspire him without encroaching on his artistic freedom. Here was a unique opportunity that seemed to answer his innermost wish.

Who shall ascend into the hill of the Lord? or who shall stand in his holy place?
PSALMS 24:3

Situated in the Judaean Hills, just west of Jerusalem, the synagogue is a simple rectangle built into the slope of a hill. Its principal square area in the center is several steps lower than the entrance and is crowned by a lantern rising high above roof level. This lantern-turret is lighted by means of twelve large windows with round arches, three on each side facing the cardinal points. Since the dawn of civilization man has been fascinated by the infinite possibilities suggested by the numbers three and four, whose sum is seven and whose product is twelve—sacred numbers governing the heavens and the earth, giving a cosmic order to both City and Temple. The number twelve has many associations, among them the twelve signs of the Zodiac which are associated in turn with the twelve tribes of Israel, the gates of Jerusalem, and the twelve carved gems of Aaron's breastplate.

In order to illuminate the synagogue both spiritually and physically, it was decided that the twelve windows, representing the twelve tribes of Israel, were to be filled with stained glass. Chagall envisioned the synagogue as "a crown offered to the Jewish Queen," the windows as jewels of translucent fire. This vision seems to be an echo of the Psalmist's rejoicing. Completely absorbed by his vision, Chagall devoted the next two years to this task. When at last he achieved results that satisfied him completely, this prodigious work was exhibited in Paris in June of 1961 and the following winter at the Museum of Modern Art in New York. In February of 1962, the stained-glass windows were finally permanently installed in the synagogue in a solemn ceremony attended by Chagall and his collaborator, Charles Marq. Today their luminous images glow from dawn to dusk beneath the sky of the Holy Land.

Despite its very exceptional subject and purpose, this great work is a fitting climax to Chagall's art, restating spiritual values that have been consistent within his complex and continuous development. In order fully to appreciate this achievement, a brief review of Chagall's life and work is necessary.

Marc Chagall was born in 1889 in Vitebsk, a provincial Russian market town that had maintained its medieval traditions. Two complementary yet distinct groups dominated the town. Both influenced Chagall's development profoundly and are reflected in his paintings: the peasants, whose roots are in the soil, and the humble craftsmen and shopkeepers of the ghetto, who ignored everything outside of their own customs and faith. Chagall's family belonged to the latter. These Jewish communities in eastern Europe were Hassidic, completely dominated by this popular and mystical religious movement which emphasized emotional expression and the belief that all actions performed religiously are holy. It was perpetuated by a rich tradition of tales and legends, in which Chagall's youth was steeped; and he has himself told of the sense of the marvelous and the religious fervor of ritual that filled his childhood. It was not long before he began to see the burning lights of Sabbath candles with the eyes of a

painter. He was driven by a talent that demanded expression in opposition to all traditions. In 1910, a crucial period for painting, he went to Paris to develop his own artistic style. Discovering Cubism and the colors of Orphism, he used them for his own aims, reversing these original purposes by thinking of them as emerging from the internal being outward, from the seen object to the psychic outpouring. Dreams and memory stimulated an imagination unfettered by rational or realistic considerations. Apollinaire recognized the supernatural as Chagall's natural environment; Breton, the metaphor as his personal idiom.

Chagall returned to Russia in 1914 and by the time he left again in 1922, having experienced enthusiasm and disillusionment and having discovered isolation to be the price of freedom, his style had matured. He had also married his fiancée, Bella, whose devotion was to remain a vital support for over twenty years. Although Paris welcomed him back with open arms, nostalgia and self-torment again came to the surface. Far from his sources of inspiration, a foreigner wherever he might live, the poet in exile has no country other than himself. "My homeland exists only in my soul" Chagall sighed, but this imaginary country did in fact exist, more pure and true than any dream. Chagall found it with his first trip to Palestine in 1931. He has said that it was the most impressive experience of his adult life—a great awakening and a revelation. Vitebsk, inscribed in his heart, and Jerusalem, with her walls of ashes and gold suspended in eternity, mingle in a single shaft of light illuminating the destiny, not only of himself, but of all humanity. His family and his ancestors throbbing in his blood and speaking through his mouth join the spiritual ancestors whose traces are revealed by his every step. Physically, morally, and poetically the truth of the Bible becomes as tangible as the land on which it is founded.

At last Chagall could illustrate the Old Testament, something that would have been impossible for him without the direct contact necessary for this kind of visionary. There are two kinds of visionaries: one who sees everything in terms of his own mystic conceptions, and the other who responds sensitively to all changes in his environment. Chagall belongs to this second type, whom one might call objective, and whose vision is the superior gift of reality.

Next he traveled in Holland and Spain to study the works of Rembrandt and El Greco, two extremes in religious painting; the first concerned entirely with the here and now, the other aspiring toward heaven. Storm clouds of a period of horror and persecution gathered, and these somber presentiments appear in his work. They almost seemed to be dictated by the Prophets who appeared not only in his engravings of this period, but also in his paintings, both of which had grown in dramatic scope. In 1935 he took a trip to Poland, this being as close as he could go to Russia, and was deeply moved by the village synagogues, soon to be systematically destroyed, that were so like those of his childhood. In 1941 he fled to the United States. His large poignant *Crucifixions* symbolize the tragic events of this period, and perhaps also reflect the personal loss of his wife, Bella.

He returned to France in 1947 and in 1949 sought the calm and light of Provence as Renoir, Bonnard, Matisse, and Picasso had done before him. His art absorbed him completely and it flowered into a magnificent paean. In the years intervening between two visits to Israel in 1951 and 1957, he again took up the Bible illustrations interrupted by the war. These monumental etchings, full of divine inspiration, retrace the legendary destiny and the epic history of Israel from Genesis to the Prophets, through the Patriarchs and the Heroes. Each picture becomes one with the event, informing the text with a solemn intimacy unknown since Rembrandt.

Never has there been greater interest in the Bible than today. There are many reasons for this: the creation of the State of Israel and the attendant vicissitudes following the horrors of war, the many archæological finds, and especially the world-shaking discovery of the Dead Sea Scrolls which suddenly brought the Bible into contact with contemporary life. Studied more and more carefully for its incomparable poetry, its literary and ethical value, it is also fervidly examined, quite apart from any religious conviction, as the fundamental revelation of the essence of being; an examination which becomes more urgent in times of crisis, confusion, and cultural change.

Committed to other things, contemporary art has abandoned this traditional source of inspiration and no longer dares to draw upon it. No period can master the full range of human potentials. By accomplishing a task that seemed either of no interest to our times or outside their scope, Chagall has transcended the limits of his century. He has unveiled possibilities unsuspected by an art that had lost touch with the Bible, and in doing so he has achieved a wholly new synthesis of

Jewish culture long ignored by painting. But his art cannot be confined to religion, for his poetry at once embraces the profane and the sacred—those elements which are so inseparable in the Old Testament itself. Nonetheless, Chagall's most moving and original contributions, what he is pleased to call "his message," are those drawn from religious or, more precisely, Biblical sources. These Biblical themes were given further development in paintings that paralleled the prints and that were to dominate his paintings from 1950 on when he was definitely settled in Vence. At this time Chagall conceived the idea of bringing his large religious paintings together in a single building able to provide an appropriate setting. He gave much thought to its thematic and architectural arrangement and felt that stained glass and ceramic murals would enliven and unify the interior space. He was able to indulge his interest in ceramics since direct contact with the material and with local craftsmen was easy. Stained glass, because of its dependence on architecture, required commissions and had to await a better opportunity.

In France the postwar revival of liturgical arts, led by the Dominicans, culminated in the Church of Assy which was consecrated in 1950. This experiment may be somewhat artificial and uneven, but it is also unique and historically of great importance because so many outstanding artists working in so many different media participated in it. Among the rather disparate windows, those by Rouault stand out with a force that remains ambiguous only because they are adaptations of paintings rather than works created specifically for stained glass. Although Rouault's paintings often supply equiv-

alent values, they do not, contrary to much current opinion, resolve the problems of stained glass. In contrast, Matisse's stained glass in the chapel at Vence and Léger's in the church at Audincourt, both dating from 1951, respond directly to the demands of the medium in their use of pure colors without gradations or ornamental installations. Their simplicity and sincerity provide felicitous solutions that hold great possibilities for the future, although in many ways they are quite unrelated to older traditions of stained glass.

After his visit to Chartres in June of 1952, Chagall was even more attracted to this medium which he felt was so suited to him, for he had studied the famous windows thoroughly from the exterior as well as from the interior. In one of the medallions of the choir, he unexpectedly recognized a kindred spirit, a prophetic coincidence which shows the extent to which his future achievements were already germinating long before there was any specific project.

The commission to decorate the baptistery at Assy with glazed-tile murals and low marble reliefs supplied Chagall with his first opportunity to experiment in this direction. This room, separated from the nave, was illuminated by two clear side-windows for which, in 1957, he designed two light grisaille figures of angels in profile, each with different attributes.

Soon after, the government bureau in charge of historic monuments broke with official practice, courageously asking three modern artists, Chagall, Roger Bissière, and Jacques Villon, to design stained glass to fill gaps in the windows of the Cathedral at Metz. Chagall was assigned two lancet windows, netted with a complex tracery, located high in the ambulatory. He could adapt his design creatively, rather than merely decoratively, to the pre-existing architecture with its medieval system of articulation between the whole and its parts because of the identification that he felt between form and idea. The idea spontaneously encompasses the form on which it is based. Moreover, what is essential in a religious program, unity of form and content, occurs on all levels—in the iconography as well as in the formal aspects. By the spring of 1958 the cartoons for these two windows were finished, with powerful Biblical scenes and figures rising in luminous tiers. Next came the actual execution in glass with its surprises and transformations. In this task Chagall had the assistance of Charles and Brigitte Marq, the proprietors of the well-known atelier Simon in Reims. These dedicated craftsmen were able to implement his ideas skillfully, and a fruitful collaboration began which was to be continued for the Jerusalem Windows. After many adjustments, one part of the Metz *Jeremiah* and *Exodus* windows was finally completed in June of 1959. Chagall said of it: "This is still only an embryo but now I am beginning to sense all the possibilities, as I did at the start of the Bible illustrations." It was exhibited in Paris where the President of Hadassah and the architect of the Hadassah-Hebrew University Medical Center saw it when they were there to see Chagall. As a result of this visit, Chagall temporarily interrupted work for the Cathedral of Metz in order to begin the Jerusalem Windows immediately.

The windows for the synagogue are approximately eleven feet high and eight feet wide, a very considerable size and much larger than anything Chagall had attempted previously, although his paintings of that period were also of larger proportions. The round arch is more reminiscent of the Romanesque than the Gothic, and the continuity of the windows in the lantern suggests a cycle. The concept of a cycle, inherent in much religious and symbolic thought, already appeared more and more consciously in Chagall's work as he developed his Biblical message. The heroic virility of the etchings for the Bible, issued in 1956, was followed by the more lyrical and feminine expression of the equally important Biblical drawings. Both series were accompanied by introspective lithographs, sometimes in black and white and sometimes in color; and these, as well as the paintings of this time, evidence a similar development. These impressive sets are no longer series or successive variations on a single theme in the Impressionistic or Romantic sense but, rather, are complete and spiritually unified organisms. Chagall's Bible illustrations are a complete historic and transcendental cycle that subordinates concrete events and persons to ultimate truths. These Biblical creations of Chagall's ultimately become a part of the Biblical world where everything has an echo, reflecting and justifying all human experience.

The essence of the Jerusalem Windows lies in color, in Chagall's magical ability to animate material and transform it into light. Words do not have the power to describe Chagall's color, its spirituality, its singing quality, its dazzling luminosity, its ever more subtle flow, and its sensitivity to the inflections of the soul and the transports of the imagination. It is simultaneously jewel-hard and foamy, reverberating and penetrating, radiating light from an unknown interior. Chagall's palette is inexhaustible, quick in sharp or subtle contrasts and, as in the latest paintings, it can enliven with infinite nuances a vast expanse dominated by a single color. Thus, the transparency and flashing brilliance of his color enabled it to be sublimated into a medium which was eminently suited to a religious subject. "Chagall reads the Bible and suddenly the passages become light," said Gaston Bachelard about the earlier drawings, and this is even more manifest in the stained glass. Stained glass, the ideal enclosure for a house of God, does in fact transform light and, by its nature and function, incarnates sacred mystery.

Like the ceramics that interested him earlier, stained glass is an art of transformation by fire, only now the material is no longer the earth but the sky. What painter has not dreamed of harvesting light, of reaping the blue and using the sky itself? In painting, Chagall has explained, the painter confronts only two artificial and rebellious elements — the canvas and the pigments, into which his talents and his spiritual powers have to breathe life. He is outnumbered two to one so that the struggle is unequal and victory difficult. When working with ceramics, however, the artist brings about the union of two natural elements, earth and fire, without thwarting either. But, if he does not approach these natural elements religiously, subordinating himself to his material, he will produce nothing but a decorative or gaping crack. If he is to achieve the celestial, having passed through hell-fire, he must possess that natural simplicity that is

the reward of age and of a religious soul at peace with the world.

The Jerusalem windows symbolize the twelve tribes of Israel who were blessed by Jacob and Moses in the celebrated lyric verses which conclude Genesis and Deuteronomy. After having blessed his grandsons, Ephraim and Manasseh, the sons of Joseph, Jacob, who is Israel, called to his side his twelve sons (who gave their names to the twelve tribes) and blessed each, calling each by name and revealing his nature and his destiny. The Hebrew benediction is inseparable from knowledge, and this knowledge transmitted from the Patriarch to his adult sons naturally became prophecy. The dying Moses repeated Jacob's solemn act and, in a somewhat different order, also blessed the twelve tribes of Israel who were about to enter the land of Canaan. During their wandering in the desert, the tribes camped in groups of three on each side of the Arc to keep watch at the four cardinal points. In the synagogue, where the windows are distributed in the same way, the tribes form a symbolic guard of honor around the tabernacle.

Mosaic law forbids the representation of the human figure, which is an image of God. Although this proscription has not always been followed faithfully, it was imposed on Chagall for the Jerusalem Windows. Realizing that he would have to conform to it, Chagall turned this obstacle to advantage. His black-and-white illustrations for the Bible make a portrait gallery, a monument to the glory of human features and expressions glimpsed at the moment that the veil of circumstance is rent. For the Jerusalem Windows, from which man is banned only to be more universally represented, Chagall has created a kingdom of stars, elements, and animals. These animals, which here are emblems of the tribes, have always been part of Chagall's personal iconography, and his incomparable illustrations of La Fontaine show how easily he moves among them. The animals of these *Fables* have their origin in the original bestiary in the first book of the Bible, the fundamental source of images and comparisons on which Jacob naturally drew to characterize his sons. All human characteristics can be transferred metaphorically to animals, and the Bible is a continuous metaphor which holds a spontaneous and natural appeal for Chagall's poetic imagination. At the end of his essay on stained glass (1937), Paul Claudel appealed to contemporary artists to revive this ancient craft and to use it for new themes. He asks, "Why not make use of all the ideas with which nature provides us—trees, foliage, the sea, all kinds of animals . . . All of them have a spiritual significance." In the Jerusalem Windows, Chagall proves the wisdom of this suggestion in the most dazzling manner.

The blessing of Ephraim and Manasseh, especially well known through Rembrandt's moving interpretation, is a recurrent artistic theme that Chagall also included among his Bible illustrations. In contrast, Jacob's second blessing, that given to his twelve sons identified with the twelve tribes, has a more strictly Jewish significance and has rarely been illustrated. The frescoes of the third-century synagogue at Dura-Europos are probably the only known example in which the two blessings are juxtaposed. At times rudimentary representations of the tribes, reduced to

their animal symbols and, therefore, easily confused with the symbols of the Zodiac, appear in Palestinian mosaics of the Greco-Roman period and in later manuscripts, marriage contracts, and cult objects. Iconographically, the breadth and unity of Chagall's windows are completely original. They integrate the traditional relation between the signs of the Zodiac and the tribes, while retaining the full cosmogonic significance inherent in both the architectural arrangement and the substance of the windows. The cycle of the tribes, which is the cycle of human generations and is associated with astrology, paths of the heavens, the turning hours and months (all equally associated with the number twelve), is swept on by the universal dynamic of light, the divine emanation of all earthly existence. Finally, the system thus established by the windows perfectly echoes the Biblical cycle. Each is an independent whole but each interacts with the others to magnify the expression of a common message: the destiny of Israel in the Promised Land and, through Israel, the destiny of man on earth.

Hundreds of thousands of people came to see these magnificent windows during the few months they were exhibited in New York and Paris. Now, in Jerusalem, they rise as a flaming crown, unhindered, toward heaven. The majestic unity and Biblical harmony of the whole can be fully appreciated only there, in that holy light. It is seven miles from Jerusalem to Ein Karem where from now on the windows will glow among the solemn crests of this landscape with its inner rhythms, circular terraces, its strength and its gentleness. There is no sudden break as one passes from the landscape into the synagogue which, in a sense, is a distillation and exaltation of its environment. On entering one sees first, in full golden glory, the window of Joseph, the favorite son, for whom:

The blessings of thy father have prevailed above the blessings of my progenitors unto the utmost bound of the everlasting hills.
GENESIS 49:26

In the thirteenth century, Abbot Suger spoke of fine gold and a profusion of jacinths, emeralds, and other precious stones, in describing the newly decorated Abbey of St. Denis, but he also meant that the actual site of the "Divine Sun" is the church. Similarly, medieval speculation that compared stained glass to the precious stones of which celestial Jerusalem was built has been taken up again in modern times by Ruskin, Proust, and Claudel. But, on reading again the passage of Exodus in which Moses receives the Holy Covenant of Sinai, one realizes that there is an even more ancient source for the Jerusalem Windows. This describes the office of the High Priest to be filled by Aaron, his sacerdotal raiments, especially:

And thou shalt make the breastplate . . . of gold, of blue, and of purple, and of scarlet . . .
And thou shalt set in it settings of stones, even four rows of stones: the first row shall be a sardius, a topaz, and a carbuncle: this shall be the first row.
And the second row shall be an emerald, a sapphire, and a diamond.
And the third row a ligure, an agate, and an amethyst.
And the fourth row a beryl, and an onyx, and a jasper: they shall be set in gold in their inclosings.
And the stones shall be with the names of the children of Israel, twelve, according to their names, like the engravings of a signet; every one with his name shall they be according to the twelve tribes.
EXODUS 28:15–21

This text is the key to the color scale of the windows, just as the verses from Genesis and Deuteronomy are the iconographic foundation of the windows. Each has its distinctive brilliance, each is a monumental jewel bearing the seal of the tribal name. On certain ones, it is even possible to read fragments of the particular blessing relating to it. The Hebraic characters are of great depth and density, being strongly inscribed in the structure of the windows. While scrupulously respecting their unchangeable form and their sacred value, Chagall admirably utilized their power of poetic and plastic suggestion to vary the degree of luminosity.

The range of colors is based on four dominant tonalities: blue, red, yellow, and green, and the windows are distributed in groups of three, like the jewels of Aaron's breastplate, in the same order used by Jacob to designate the tribes. Thus, on the east wall there is Reuben, on a light-blue ground, Simeon, on a dark-blue ground, and Levi, on a clear-yellow ground. On the south wall, we see the garnet-red of Judah, together with the more cheerful vermilion of Zebulun and the soft green of Issachar. The west wall holds Dan, on a blue ground, Gad on a dark-green ground, and Asher, again on a soft-green ground. Naphtali, dominated by lemon yellow, Joseph harmonizing in golden yellow, and Benjamin on a bright-blue ground, are located on the north wall. Each window is a translucent painting, modulated by light and affected by the unequal radiance of the colors. Thus, yellow is the color which is least radiant, and blue the color which is most radiant. Blue, the color of the heavens, is the light of all the windows giving relative values to all the other tones, thereby providing essential stability and, at the same time, permitting infinite nuances. This is why four windows are of a generally blue dominant tone, while only two are dominated by red. The basic harmony between the blues and the reds, interrupted by intermediate violet tones—sapphires and rubies punctuated by amethysts—balances the wonderful audacity of three green windows against three yellow ones—emeralds and chrysolites with topaz reflections.

As in his printmaking, Chagall is not conspicuous here for any technical innovation. He challenges the oversimplified modern processes, such as great slabs of glass, and he adheres to the time-tested traditions which he has assimilated, reviving their secrets by the irrepressible power of his inspiration. His vision pervades the creation; the total immersion of the poet in his subject overcomes the resistance of the material, controlling it with absolute mastery, as is natural to an artisan. "Expert worker in his art and skillful magician"—never has this definition of the artist according to Isaiah been better confirmed.

This book allows us to follow, for each of the windows, what Chagall, until now, has never revealed for any of his works—the mysteries of development and the successive phases, from the first rough sketches with their flashing, spontaneous inspiration through the double series of designs where rhythms and colors are established, to the final achievement. The creative imagination is caught from the moment it takes flight and followed through successive stages of its development.

As both physical and metaphysical light, the window is a sacred vessel, a cosmic vehicle, carrying infinite significance. The supernatural art of Chagall finds there, in the magnificence of age, a rare opportunity of accomplishment whose influence is echoed in the development of his current painting. The birds, the fish, the lambs are his chosen animals, creatures of a fantastic bestiary. The symbols of the Law, such as the Torah, the Star, the ram's horn (*shofar*), the candles and their seven-branched candelabrum (*menorah*), the sea, the firmament and its "enormous lights," the earth with its vegetation varied by the seasons and the climates, the confused images of Jerusalem and Vitebsk, all the familiar symbols of his work carried along in the cycle of elements and stars are here rejoined, almost by osmosis, with the Biblical symbols. The freest and most individual imagination is also the one most faithful to the poetic truth of the Scriptures.

Rather than tending toward decorative and picturesque representation, the absence of the human figure gives majestic and universal resonance to the purity of the fundamental symbols. Three principal windows, among the most intense in color, form a magnetic triangle at the interior of the crown— from the center of the north wall to either side of the south wall. At the apex of this triangle, the human presence is suggested in a religious context by the priest's hands holding the ram's horn (*shofar*), symbol of the New Year, above the bow of Joseph, raising to the sky the sparkling crown of Judah, and blessing the enchanted countryside of Issachar. The two trees of Genesis, one of which is the tree of life, appear in most of the windows as do the four heraldic animals of the synagogue or their equivalents, the dove, the lion, the eagle, and the stag, bounding off into the four corners of space. Finally, open and glowing eyes, most lively and precious of gems, mirrors of the soul and flowers of light, glisten everywhere. Man, therefore, is represented by his essential powers: sight and touch.

Form, color, and content, sublimated by light, victorious over weight and opacity, coincide perfectly within the unity of individual windows and in the whole cycle. The poetic spell is total and the spiritual meaning, so intimately connected with Biblical sources, still allows a margin of personal interpretation. The metaphors of the two blessings become luminous images which are directly expressive. The strength of Reuben in his pure cerulean blue is conveyed by the emergence of the solar disc, the proud flight of the birds, and the jubilation of the fish. A nocturnal and malignant blue weighs heavily on the dispersed cities and on the violent universe of Simeon from which wounded doves take flight. The candles blaze around the Torah on the sacerdotal window of Levi, light yellow with glimmers of rose. Judah crouches like a lion in his crimson splendor, under the royal crown. Only in this window did Chagall wish to sign his name in Hebraic characters, for this window is truly supernatural and, through the mystical crown, it symbolizes all the windows: Chagall's crown for Israel. The ship of Zebulun sails in a tumultuous red softened by the violet reflections of a sunset on the water. Issachar is an indolent ass sleeping in the peace of his open fields, in this window of spring, the most tender if not the most beautiful of the series. It is one of the few windows ever made based on the dominant calm of the color green, and on the subtle and perilous relationship between green and blue, ". . . of which," said Viollet-le-Duc, "we can find examples only in certain Persian enamels and in the flowers of our fields. Everyone has been able to contemplate the gentle harmony of blue flax against the green grass." Dan, the judge of his people, is a vermilion lion cub springing against a background of ultramarine blue; he is an adder in the path that bites horses' heels. Gad, a somber green clashing against funereal red, is the terrifying window of war, peopled by animals which are more aggressive and monstrous than those of Bosch. Asher, on the other hand, where a rainbow of colors gleams against an emerald background, displays an oriental luxuriance. Naphtali, a hind let loose and surfeited with favors, stretches out in the sunny light. The color yellow increases and culminates in the window of Joseph, whose strong bow is stretched out over the fruitful soil. Finally, Benjamin's multi-colored window, dominated by blue, assembles all the tribes in an indefinite gyration. The last to be named by Jacob, Benjamin marches at the head of the processions:

There is little Benjamin with their ruler, the princes of Judah and their council, the princes of Zebulun, and the princes of Naphtali.
PSALMS 68:27

These windows are discussed in more detail on the pages reserved for the plates. The explanation is sometimes difficult and no doubt useless, for no

xvi

commentary can exhaust the richness and the often polyvalent profundity of the symbols. It is better to abandon oneself naïvely to their magical charm and to read once more in the Psalms those verses which may correspond to them and better situate their climate. Thus, for Gad's somber and jagged-looking window:

My soul is among the lions: and I lie even among them . . . whose teeth are spears and arrows, and their tongues a sharp sword.
PSALMS 57:4

or, on the contrary, for the peaceful splendor of Issachar and Asher:

Thou crownest the year with thy goodness; and thy paths drop fatness.
They drop upon the pastures of the wilderness: and the little hills rejoice on every side.
The pastures are clothed with flocks; the valleys also are covered over with corn; they shout for joy, they also sing.
PSALMS 65:11–13

One would also like to call on poets who were friends of Chagall's and who best knew how to praise him, from the divinatory cry of Blaise Cendrars:

Chagall
Chagall
Among the ladders of light

or the fittingly luminous vision of Apollinaire:

A day made of fragments of mauves yellows blues greens and reds

to Eluard's quatrain which seemed to prophecy the windows:

The gold of the grass the lead of the sky
Separated by flames of blue
With health with dew
The blood is iridescent the heart rings.

If Chagall's Biblical illustrations and the windows of Metz call to mind the Gothic style, the windows of Jerusalem evoke the power and monumental majesty of Romanesque masterpieces. Henri Focillon, quoted by Raïssa Maritain in her essay on Chagall, wrote, "The Romanesque period is dominated by visionaries. They communicate to it their superhuman instincts, their taste for hidden things and for supernatural truths. They wrench it from the commonplace, from normal proportions, from the balance of reason, they revive the frenzied epic of St. John the Divine, but they are not content to illustrate these texts of fire, they make them the subject of a strange and most personal dream." Drawing on the same sources and gifted with the same inspiration, but with the confusion of modern times and without the support of a collective faith, Chagall has built by himself the Temple of Light where East and West are united; he has raised his personal fantasy to the level of a myth and to sacred dimensions. The "frenzied epic of John" concludes with the dazzling vision of a celestial Jerusalem, a city of pure gold resembling clear glass, built on a perfect square, girdled with a wall of jasper, pierced by twelve gates, three on the east, three on the north, three on the west, three on the south, on which are inscribed the names of Jacob's twelve sons, the twelve tribes of Israel.

Like the seer of Patmos, Chagall aspires, after the cataclysms, to the fullness of redeemed humanity, but his inspiration is concentrated here on the Old Testament and its heroic exploits. A sovereign artistic monument and a truly universal religious message restrained by no limitations of confessed faith, the windows of Jerusalem, beyond the Judaic spirituality with which they are impregnated, propose against the poverty and mutilation of our era, a complete humanism, new and eternal.

"And this, which today is called sacred art," declared Chagall the morning of the inauguration, "I carried out by thinking equally of the great ancient creations of the Semitic peoples of this region. And I hope that thus I am holding out a hand to friends of culture, to poets and artists of neighboring countries and of all countries." The fact remains that his sublime masterpiece was conceived especially for its site in the land of the Prophets, to live and shine in the Biblical light which is unlike any other. For, as Moses proclaimed at the end of his benedictions: *The fountain of Jacob shall be upon a land of corn and wine; also his heavens shall drop down dew.*
DEUTERONOMY 33:28

Each of the twelve stained-glass windows

reproduced on the following pages

is preceded by a preparatory set of drawings and models

whose number, media, dimensions

and order of presentation

are exactly the same in the sequence

of each tribe and are arranged as follows:

	Height	Width
First sketch, pencil, pen and India ink	7⅞ ×	5⅞ "
Preparatory drawing, India ink and wash	15⅞ ×	11⅝ "
First color sketch, India ink and watercolor	7⅞ ×	5⅞ "
Small model, gouache and collage	8⅝ ×	18⅞ "
Final model, gouache and collage	16½ ×	12½ "

Finished window . . . .   133 × 98¾ "

REUBEN

Eldest son of Jacob and Leah, Reuben lost the patrimony due to him because he had soiled the couch of Bilhah, servant of Rachel, concubine of Jacob, and mother of Dan and Naphtali. He dissuaded his brothers from killing Joseph and proposed his sons as hostages to save Benjamin. Generous, but hot-tempered, "unstable as water," his powers will be moderated for fear of his excesses.

This first window opens the cycle with a harmony as imposing and pure as the very breath of creation. Cerulean blue laid on a white base gleams majestically, evoking the limpidity of air, the transparent foaming of the sea, the amplitude and freshness of a newly

created Biblical space. The solar disc, with its vast extending rays, contains the Hebraic characters, in themselves sacred, which bear witness to the Divine presence identified with cosmic light:

Who hath measured the waters in the hollow of his hand, and meted out heaven with the span, and comprehended the dust of the earth in a measure . . .
ISAIAH 40:12

With limitless vitality, four birds in the air and four fish in the water take full possession of their respective elements:

Let Reuben live, and not die; and let not his men be few.

says the blessing of Moses (Deuteronomy 33:6). At the lower right flowers whose blazing reds make the surrounding blues sing are perhaps the sensual transposition of mandrakes, the love apples of The Song of Songs which Reuben found in the fields and offered to his mother Leah (Genesis 30:14). Above, in a marvelous complementary green space (these greens and reds are echoed in the sky in the plumage of the birds), are tiny, luminous sheep, an allusion to the pastoral condition of the nomadic tribe which grazed its flocks beyond the Jordan river. Particularly noteworthy are the beauty of the underwater background, the strange rose and violet glimmers like a reflection under the central fish parallel to the horizon line, and the infinite delicacy of the water plants. The very supple shapes of the glass fragments and the often curvilinear tracery of the leading combines with the luminous fluidity of the color which is magnificently heightened by accents of grisaille and by airy clear spaces.

1

Reuben, thou art my firstborn,
my might, and the beginning of my strength,
the excellency of dignity, and the excellency of power:
Unstable as water.

GENESIS 49:3–4

SIMEON

Simeon and Levi, often associated with the Gemini of the Zodiac, had been the protagonists in a reprisal to avenge the dishonor of their sister Dinah, who had been seduced by Shechem, son of Hamor. By a ruse they massacred Shechem and his men, pillaged his city and the countryside, captured the women and children, the livestock and all their goods (Genesis 34).

Thus, the blessing is conditional and supposes an alternative. Jacob stigmatizes the shared violence of the two brothers:

For in their anger they slew a man, and in their selfwill they digged down a wall.

and announces that they will not have their own lands in the division of Palestine:

I will divide them in Jacob, and scatter them in Israel.
GENESIS 49:6–7

However, the violence of Simeon is absolved and justified in the prayer of Judith, and in the following window we shall see the exceptional condition to which Levi was raised. In order to separate the ultimate destiny of the two tribes, Chagall isolates the name of Simeon in the upper right-hand sphere and places across the bottom of the window the transcription of the quotation from Jacob which also contains the name of Levi.

After the clear blue of Reuben, fresh as a bubbling stream and pure as the sunrise, the somber blue of Simeon establishes a grave and nocturnal atmosphere. The achievement of this dominant tone, with which all the blues concur, is a technical success. Similarly, the insertion of three multicolored spheres on the surface and in the dark mass of the window is a plastic marvel. The lower central sphere represents the earth, with its division between day and night. On the right a winged bull flies away. Between the two upper spheres which represent planets—one the color of flame and deserted, the other mauve and flowering—is a turbulent space in which the messenger of war and death advances—the horse of combat whose warlike ardor has been celebrated by Job (Job 39:19–25). This is also the mount, or the symbolic emblem, of the Gemini. Its splendid green foresection is complemented by the bloody red of the two wounded doves. In the panels at the bottom, just above the Hebrew letters, numerous houses treated in the manner of cubist fragmentation are perhaps meant to evoke the seventeen cities attributed to Simeon in the Negev region, at the very interior of the territory of Judah (Joshua 19:9). Notice, in the lower left, the modulation of the blues, the rhythm of the leading, the lighting of the Hebraic characters, the eye inscribed in a triangle, the look of a watchful God . . .

Weapons of violence are their swords.
Because in their fury they slew men,
in their willfulness they hamstrung oxen.
Cursed be their fury because it is violent.

LEVI

Simeon is omitted in the blessings of Moses, who reserves his words for a solemn blessing on Levi. Moses himself belonged to the descendants of Levi, who redeemed the sin of their ancestor (see the preceding window) and saw themselves consecrated to holy offices. The third book of the Pentateuch, *Leviticus,* constitutes the sacerdotal code of major importance for these people whose whole being is founded on an Alliance with God. The religious functions are assumed by priests (*Kohanim*), obedient to the Holy Law, who are assisted by the Levites. The first high priest was Aaron, brother of Moses. Entirely devoted to the service of the sanctuary and to the office of mediation between God and the people, Levi had no earthly inheritance and practically ceased to exist as a tribe. The number twelve will be maintained,

however, by division of the Tribe of Joseph into two tribes: Ephraim and Manasseh.

The color yellow, solar exaltation and divine light, magnifies the sacred character of this window. It becomes more dazzling and pure placed as it is between the somber blue of Simeon and the deep red of Judah. The Tablets of the Law, crimson and violet, carry, with the beginning of the following verse, the central verse of Moses' blessing which sums up the functions of the priests:

They shall teach Jacob thy judgments, and Israel thy law: they shall put incense before thee, and whole burnt sacrifice upon thine altar.
DEUTERONOMY 33:10

Around the Torah burn "like flamboyant jacinthes," according to Chagall, the candles which generate a mystic light. The two objects in the form of a candelabrum in front of the altar suggest, in addition, a possible allusion to the cup of the *kiddush* and the candlestick of the *havdala.* The four heraldic animals of the synagogue, embodying religious spirituality, whose bright colors emerge from the deep yellow background, frolic around a vase of offerings filled with flowers and fruits as well as around the star, emblem of David, the symbolic hexagram which has become the widespread symbol of Judaism today. Its presence is anachronistic, but it is charged with an intense beauty.

Chagall has magnificently animated the yellow ground, so difficult to make lustrous, by a continuous vibration of little details painted with lightness and delicacy, like oriental embroidery, and numerous accents of light. Notice the use of silvered yellow and, in a portion of the stag, the Persian rose-gold.

They have observed thy word,
and kept thy covenant.
They shall teach Jacob thy judgments,
and Israel thy law.

DEUTERONOMY 33:9–10

JUDAH

Because of the grave sins committed by his elder brothers, Reuben, Simeon, and Levi, Judah, the fourth son of Jacob and Leah, became the privileged recipient of the blessing which carried with it a messianic oracle. The pre-eminence of Judah is linked with the glory of David, King of Judah, also elected King of Israel by the other tribes and who, having conquered the reputedly impregnable Canaanite citadel of Jerusalem, made it—by decisive choice—the capital. He solemnly carried there the Ark of the Covenant for which he planned a Temple which was later built by his son Solomon. The nation created by David did not survive the death of Solomon. Although Palestine was divided into two kingdoms, Israel in the north and Judah in the south, the prestige of the Temple confirmed Jerusalem as the Holy City:

. . . But he chose the tribe of Judah, the mount Zion which he loved . . . , he chose David also his servant . . . , he brought him to feed Jacob his people, and Israel his inheritance.

PSALMS 78:68–71

The traditional lion of Judah is crouched in sovereign majesty against the ramparts of Jerusalem. In a ritual gesture of blessing, two hands of a priest raise the royal crown, glittering with gems. The upper portion of this window shows with what inspired fervor it has been painted, as though by a mystical jeweler:

For thou preventest him with the bless-ings of goodness: thou settest a crown of pure gold on his head.

PSALMS 21:3

The dominant crimson color, obtained by the combination of at least four different reds, gives to the stained glass a deep glow which is accentuated by the masterful modulation of the shadows and lights with great engraved spaces of clear glass. This red color punctuated with white symbolizes power, the blood of battles, and the "blood of grapes"; it is in direct agreement with the two final verses of the blessing, illustrating early life in Judaea, where there was an abundance of wine and milk:

Binding his foal unto the vine, and his ass's colt unto the choice vine; he washed his garments in wine, and his clothes in the blood of grapes;
His eyes shall be red with wine, and his teeth white with milk.

GENESIS 49:11–12

Chagall wished to engrave and sign his own name in Hebraic characters on this window alone, with its particular significance. It is also possible to recognize in the mysterious green and blue initials to the left and right of the lion, and in the drawing of the clear upper panel which encloses the hands in benediction, the three letters which compose, in Hebrew, the name of the crown, *keter.*

Judah is invested with a great importance in the Christian religion and its iconography. The Apocalypse (5:5) designates Christ as "lion of the tribe of Judah" and "offspring of David."

Judah is a lion's whelp.
The sceptre shall not depart from Judah,
nor a lawgiver from between his feet.

GENESIS 49:9–10

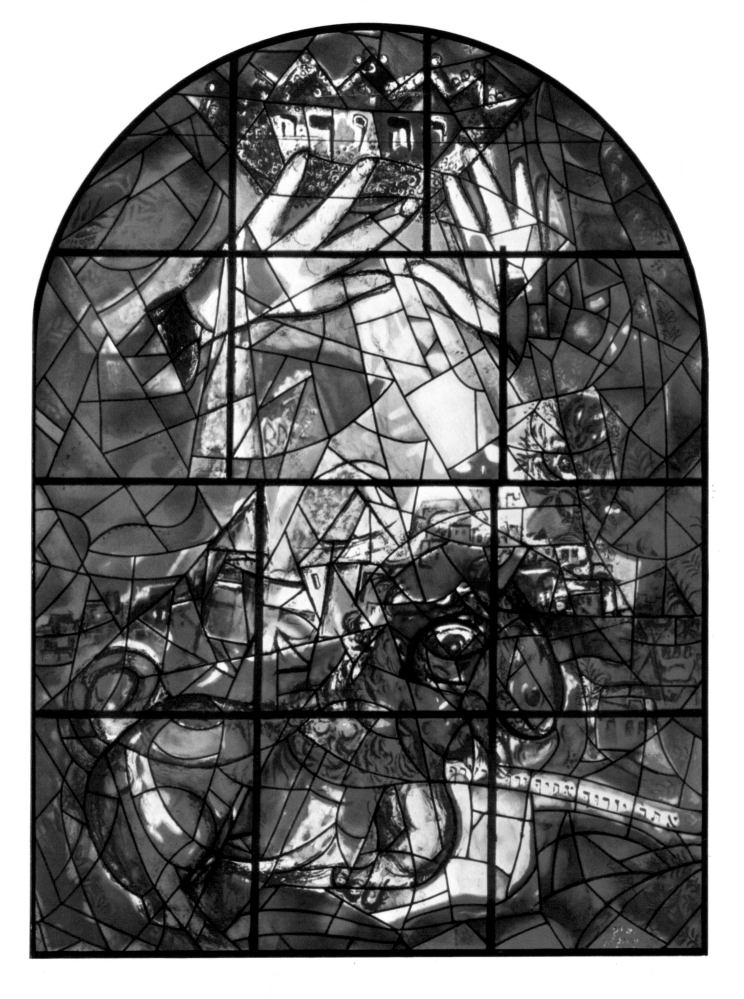

ZEBULUN

Issachar and Zebulun, the two youngest children of Leah, are joined together in the blessing of Moses who assigns to the two tribes a prosperous destiny. Issachar in his tents and Zebulun in his "going out," in the course of which they will "suck of the abundance of the seas." Jacob blessed Zebulun and Issachar separately, giving the priority to Zebulun, although he was the younger. He predicted for him a maritime vocation, and designated him as "an haven of ships; and his border shall be unto Zion." The ship is the usual symbol for Zebulun; but, in reality, Zebulun occupied a continental territory rather small but fertile in lower Galilee and the plain of Esdraelon, between Mount Carmel and Mount Tabor. It was separated from the lake of Tiberiad by Naphtali and from the Mediterranean by Asher; but it was crossed by very active com- mercial routes and had access to the Phoenician ports, of which the most important was Zidon, mentioned several times in Homer, the Bible, and Babylonian manuscripts.

Against the cadmium red background, whites gleam and greens and blues ring in contrast. The dizzying power of this window flashes from the middle of the south wall, between the tender green of Issachar and the somber crimson of Judah. The two splendid fish, composed of multicolored pieces of glass and arranged at the center in a movement which is wedded to the arched form of the window, evoke the fish depicted on ancient Palestinian mosaics—either as signs of the Zodiac or as religious symbols. The bond of rushing water and fish as symbolic of resurrection predates Christianity. Furthermore, the fish—without sectarian significance—has been one of the most frequent motifs of popular Jewish art in eastern Europe since the seventeenth century; and it recurs constantly, in multiple associations and contexts, in the personal iconography of Chagall.

The violent symphony of red tones diminishes toward the lower right into the inexpressible sweetness of a sunset casting its luminous reflections on the water. The depths are marvelously highlighted by the technique of scraping off paint with the tip of a brush or even with a finger, to form a sort of oriental damask. Admire, as in the under-water background of the Reuben window, the transparency in depth and the extreme delicacy of the water plants which have an almost magical value. Notice also, in the upper portion of the window, the masterful chromatic and plastic use of the characters which form, in Hebrew, the name Zebulun.

Zebulun shall dwell at the haven of the sea;
and he shall be for an haven of ships;
and his border shall be unto Zidon.

GENESIS 49:13

ISSACHAR

Palestine. The abundance of goods which this tribe possessed, the flat and naturally defenseless character of the countryside, exposed it to enemy incursions and to a servile position which it easily accepted. This is made clear by the blessing of Jacob:

Issachar is a strong ass crouching down between two burdens: And he saw that rest was good, and the land that it was pleasant; and bowed his shoulder to bear, and became a servant unto tribute.

GENESIS 49:14–15

After the blinding effulgence of Judah and Zebulun, the harmony of this window rests on a dominant light green, tender and calm, which is the very expression of spring and of paradisial joy. The principal produce of Issachar, the vine, so often celebrated in the Bible as the principle of fertility and, especially, as the mystic symbol of Israel itself (Isaiah 5:1–12; Psalms 80:8–15, etc.), circles in a continuous garland around the window. The lovingly painted trees and plants, in which birds perch, exalt the luxuriant vegetation. The robust ass, symbolizing the tribe, indolently savors the splendor of his country. The weight which he ought to bear as the tribute of a slave is sufficiently light for Chagall to represent it with humor by means of a tiny bird, outlined in black. One notices, in near transparency, a prosperous village (in this section, notice the counterpoint of grisaille and leading) and flocks spread out over the countryside. At the center, two hands in blessing (in a non-ritual gesture) inscribe, under a triangle of light where the text of the first verse of Jacob's blessing is written in Hebrew, the two most intense color accents of the composition: emerald and carmine.

After a period of sterility, Leah, thanks to the mandrakes brought to her by her eldest son Reuben (see the following windows), conceived by Jacob a fifth child, Issachar. The tribe of Issachar, bounded on the north by Zebulun and Naphtali, on the east by the Jordan River, received for its portion the largest part of the fertile plain of Esdraelon at the foot of Mount Tabor. This was watered by the Qishon and, as a land of travel routes, was the strategic key to

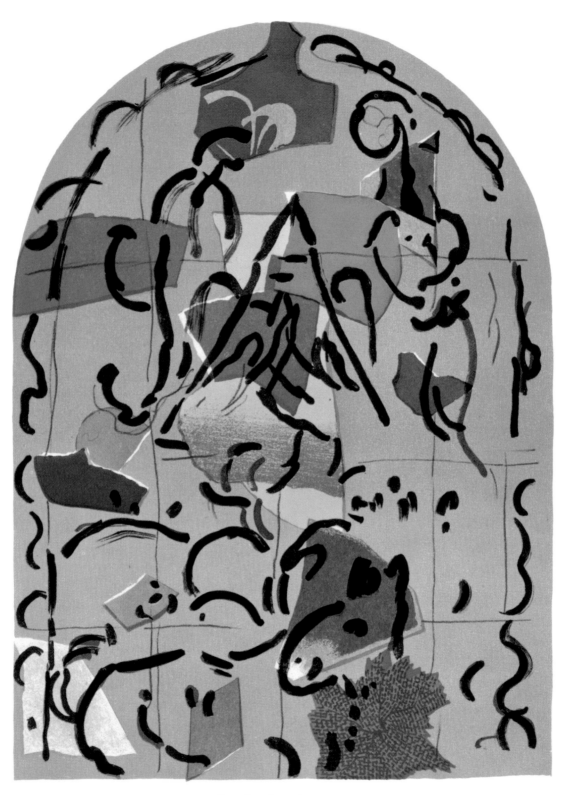

Issachar is a strong ass
couching down between two burdens:
And he saw that rest was good,
and the land that it was pleasant.

GENESIS 49:14–15

DAN

First child of Bilhah, Rachel's servant, Dan signifies judge and, to emphasize the fact that this distant tribe belonged to the ethnic group of the sons of Israel, Jacob said:

Dan shall judge his people, as one of the tribes of Israel . . .
GENESIS 49:16

In the theoretic apportionment of Palestine, Dan received a plot, between Ephraim and Judah, which included a coastal strip around the famous port of Jaffa. But it did not have access to the plain, for the Amorites drove his tribe back against the mountain. Being numerous and lacking sufficient space, the tribe then undertook a long and difficult expedition, recounted in detail in Judges (18), in order to acquire new territory in the northeast region of Palestine near the source of the Jordan River. It destroyed the primitive city of Laish and built in its place a new capi-

tal, named after the tribal ancestor Dan. It thus bordered on the Bashan plateau, which Manasseh inhabited, hence the metaphor of Moses:

. . . Dan is a lion's whelp: he shall leap from Bashan.
DEUTERONOMY 33:22

A majestic three-branched candelabrum forms the central axis of this predominantly dark-blue composition. It rises both as the tree of life and as the tree of justice, and perhaps also as a symbol of sovereignty. Its flaming lights create an area of diffused yellow between the red animals, compensated by a green space below. Around the candelabrum twines the horned viper, dangerous serpent of the desert, which strikes suddenly at anything which comes near and makes horses rear back in fright:

Dan shall be a serpent by the way, an adder in the path, that biteth the horse heels . . .
GENESIS 49:17

Between the branches of the candelabrum rises a vermilion lion cub, in a traditional pose. His right paw, which becomes the hand of justice, holds the sword of war, which also serves as the beam for a scales. "And thou, son of man, take thee a sharp knife, take thee a barber's razor . . . then take thee balances to weigh, and divide the hair." (Ezekiel 5:1.)

If I whet my glittering sword, and mine hand take hold on judgment . . .
DEUTERONOMY 32:41

The right side shows bouquets and trees painted with Chagall's habitual tenderness, as well as variations in transparency and luminosity of the blues, and the walls and dome of the city drawn in full light.

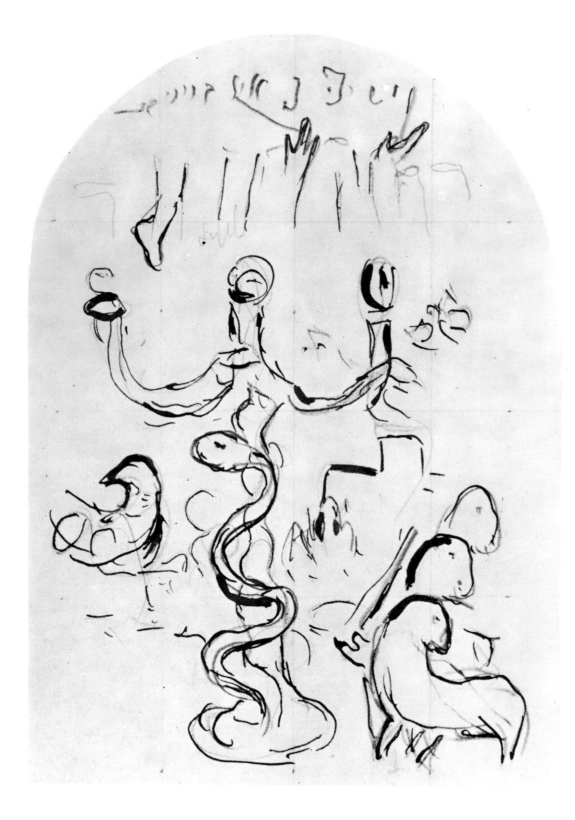

Dan shall judge his people,
as one of the tribes of Israel.
Dan shall be a serpent by the way,
an adder in the path.

GAD

First son of Zilpah, Leah's servant, Gad is the ancestor of the tribe that received the land of Transjordan, between Reuben to the south and the demi-tribe of Manasseh to the north. Gad's tribe took possession of its domain, however, only after having helped the other tribes to conquer the land of Canaan. It inhabited the fertile region of Galilee, "propitious for flocks," and, unceasingly defending itself against waves of nomadic invasions, came to fulfill the blessing of Jacob:

Gad, a troop shall overcome him: but he shall overcome at the last.
GENESIS 49:19

Moses celebrated the faithfulness to duty of this tribe, which was unjustly accused of idolatry, and called attention to its formidable violence in combat:

. . . He dwelleth as a lion, and teareth the arm with the crown of the head.
DEUTERONOMY 33:20

In fact, the Gadites were famous warriors. Certain among them joined David "into the hold to the wilderness," among the Philistines at Ziklag. "Men of might, and men of war fit for the battle, that could handle shield and buckler, whose faces were like the faces of lions, and were as swift as the roes upon the mountains . . . These were the sons of Gad, captains of the host: one of the least was over an hundred, and the greatest over a thousand." (I Chronicles 12:8–14.)

Situated in the middle of the west wall of the lantern, across from the nocturnal and funereal window of Simeon, this window—more terrifying still—is an apocalyptic vision of war. The crowned royal eagle high on the left, holding a large shield in the form of a solar disc and, to the right, the horse, also crowned, charging irresistibly with a sword—which symbolizes the tribe—are driving back a host of raging beasts as monstrous as the hybrids of Bosch. The composition, different from that of the other windows, is an accumulation of shattered fragments, an ensemble of scattered pieces masterfully reassembled. The colors, a dominant somber green punctuated by a bloody red, glare in perpetual dissonance and depict, together with the sharp ruptures of the design, all the tumult and ferocity of battle, the sinister clash of weapons thrust forward on every side. A little plant life, preserved from the general disaster, is wilting in the lower left-hand section of the window. The section with the tower rising in a green and blue glow underlines the intensity of the contrasts, the richness of transitions, and the forceful use of grisaille and open spaces of light.

Gad, a troop shall overcome him:
but he shall overcome at the last.

GENESIS 49:19

ASHER

Full brother to Gad, Asher is the second son of Zilpah, Leah's servant. His name signifies happiness, prosperity. The tribe, famous for its wisdom and the beauty of its women, received the most fertile territory, on the Mediterranean coast between Mount Carmel and Phœnicia. Its principal cultivation was the olive tree, symbol of opulence and of joy, and it was able to provide oil for all of Israel. From this comes the blessing of Moses:

Let Asher be blessed with children; let him be acceptable to his brethren, and let him dip his foot in oil.

DEUTERONOMY 33:24

Jacob's blessing suggests abundance and the oriental succulence of a king's banquet:

Out of Asher his bread shall be fat, and he shall yield royal dainties.

GENESIS 49:20

If Gad is the devastating window of war, Asher is the luxuriant window of peace and of happiness which follows in the wake of peace. The tribe did not participate in the battle against Sisera:

Asher continued on the sea shore, and abode in his breaches.

JUDGES 5:17

On the ceremonial table burns the seven-branched candelabrum (*menorah*) described in Exodus (25:31–40), whose perpetual flame was to be maintained with "pure oil olive beaten for the light" (Exodus 27:20). One knows that this light of many attributes, cosmological and mystical (Tree of Life, Divine Light, glow of planets, etc.), symbolizes Judaism, as the cross symbolizes Christianity, and is the most frequent motif in the decoration of synagogues, tombs, and religious objects. The fifth vision of Zechariah (4:1–14), illustrated by Chagall in his earlier Bible drawings, is of a candelabrum between two olive trees.

The dominant tonality is a soft green like that of Issachar, often lightened to white or clear glass, on which vibrates a quivering drawing of luminous color. Blue fused with yellow was especially made for this tone, which is also found in two other windows, Issachar and Gad. In its double thickness it gives green, but the union of two colors makes possible marvelous and subtle transitions from blue to green and to yellow. Birds are traditionally associated with the richness of plant life and the fruits that they pilfer. Above the central crowned eagle flies the messenger dove of peace carrying, like Noah's dove, an olive branch (Genesis 8:11). The two-handled pitcher to the left of the candelabrum develops a bird's head (vases and also human beings with heads of animals are frequently found in ancient oriental and in medieval art), and one can see a hand at its side, under the disc of a multicolored planet whose turning motion affects the whole composition.

Out of Asher his bread shall be fat,
and he shall yield royal dainties.

GENESIS 49:20

NAPHTALI

Naphtali, full brother to Dan, is the second son of Bilhah, Rachel's servant. The territory of northern Palestine assigned to this tribe included, around the lake of Tiberiad, "the district of nations," that is, Galilee, a region devastated and enslaved by the Assyrian army but for which Isaiah predicted a messianic liberation (Isaiah 9) and which, according to Matthew, was the site of the ministry of Jesus. Naphtali responded to the call of Gideon (Judges 7:23) and, with Zebulun, marched at the head of a campaign against Sisera (Judges 5:18). The blessing of Moses is simple as well as complete:

O Naphtali, satisfied with favour, and full with the blessing of the Lord . . .
DEUTERONOMY 33:23

Jacob compared Naphtali to a "hind let loose: he giveth goodly words" (Genesis 49:21). Job questioned himself on the conception and mysterious birth of the hind which is often mentioned in the Psalms and The Song of Songs as a symbol of agility, of grace, and of amorous tenderness.

Like the window of Levi, the dominant tonality of this window is a lemon yellow, fused over light gray. As early as the treatise of Theophile, stained-glass makers have expressed a legitimate hesitation to use yellow over a large surface because the color is not luminous and everything inscribed on it becomes dense. Despite this ancient mistrust, Chagall wished to keep to his plan and make three monumental yellow windows, of which the most difficult was undoubtedly this one. The red plastic mass of the stag was remade three times before it achieved its splendid equilibrium in the light web of glass. The silvered yellow is visible in the three-colored pieces used in the body of the animal. In contrast to the position of the ass of Issachar, or the lion of Judah, the hind rests at the foot of a height to which houses cling. The branches of his supple blue antlers stretch out like the flames of a candelabrum. Above, separated by a luxuriantly green and tender blue tree, stands a great bird, dark red and dark blue, possibly an eagle, which is traditionally connected with the tree of life, or possibly a cock. The cock, symbol of vigilance and of resurrection, is a frequent motif in the recent painting of Chagall and sometimes, as here, is associated, among trees or flowers, with other animals: asses, stags, horses. The bird's gesture of menace or defiance might perhaps be an allusion to the origin of the word Naphtali, which means "I have fought." A decoration of the Coptic monastery of Baouit, clarified by its inscription, shows a gazelle, symbol of the soul (like the hind), attacked by a lion, symbol of the devil (the eagle has the same ambivalent powers as the lion), near a tree of life which represents Paradise.

Naphtali is a hind let loose:
he giveth goodly words.

GENESIS 49:21

JOSEPH

Child of her old age and first-born of Rachel, Joseph was the favorite son of Jacob. He aroused the jealousy of his brothers who plotted to kill him, and then sold him to a caravan of merchants traveling to Egypt. His long and romantic story, the details of which comprise the last chapters of Genesis, has become familiar through numerous artistic cycles that have been created to illustrate it. Chagall devoted eight plates of his illustrated Bible to Joseph's story. The tribe of Joseph was divided between his two sons, Ephraim and Manasseh, whom Jacob blessed even before blessing his own sons. Joseph and Judah were the two privileged sons: Judah receiving the scepter and Joseph receiving the patrimony of the eldest which had been forfeited by Reuben.

Jacob and Moses reserved for Joseph the longest, as well as the most solemn, blessing, calling

. . . on the crown of the head of him that was separate from his brethren.
GENESIS 49:26

the fullness of a cosmic favor which embraces the Heavens, the Earth, and the Underworld.

The golden harmony of this triumphant window, brightly shining directly opposite the entrance, across from the brilliant red of Zebulun, is the result of two orange ochres fused to white and yellow. The vast extent of such a color, as sumptuous as it is re-bellious, is enlivened by a continuous pulsation of the ground, a tremulous punctuation by the grisaille which is arranged in gentle links to capture the light. The rhythm of the drawing is a succession of spirals and enveloping curves. According to the metaphor of Jacob, spreading out on the left is the "fruitful bough" whose "branches run over the wall." In the mighty tree, whose multicolored spirals are laden with fruit, nests a crowned dove. The name Joseph is inscribed in a circle above it. To the right of the bird, "the strong bow" mentioned by Jacob and the poised arrow protect the flocks and the abundance of earthly blessings invoked by Moses:

Blessed of the Lord be his land, for the precious things of heaven, for the dew, and for the deep that coucheth beneath. And for the precious fruits brought forth by the sun, and for the precious things put forth by the moon. And for the chief things of the ancient mountains, and for the precious things of the lasting hills. And for the precious things of the earth and fulness thereof . . .
DEUTERONOMY 33:13–16

At the top of the window, illustrating the Messianic meaning of Joseph, two hands carefully hold the trumpet of the ram's horn (*shofar*), announcer of freedom and salvation which is sounded on rare occasions—most notably the purifying feasts of the New Year and the Day of Atonement. The *shofar* is often represented on ancient funerary monuments, together with other ritual objects. The hands associated with the *shofar,* as they are here, appear on recent Jewish tombs (eighteenth and nineteenth centuries) in the Ukraine and eastern Europe.

Joseph is a fruitful bough,
even a fruitful bough by a well;
whose branches run over the wall.

GENESIS 49:22

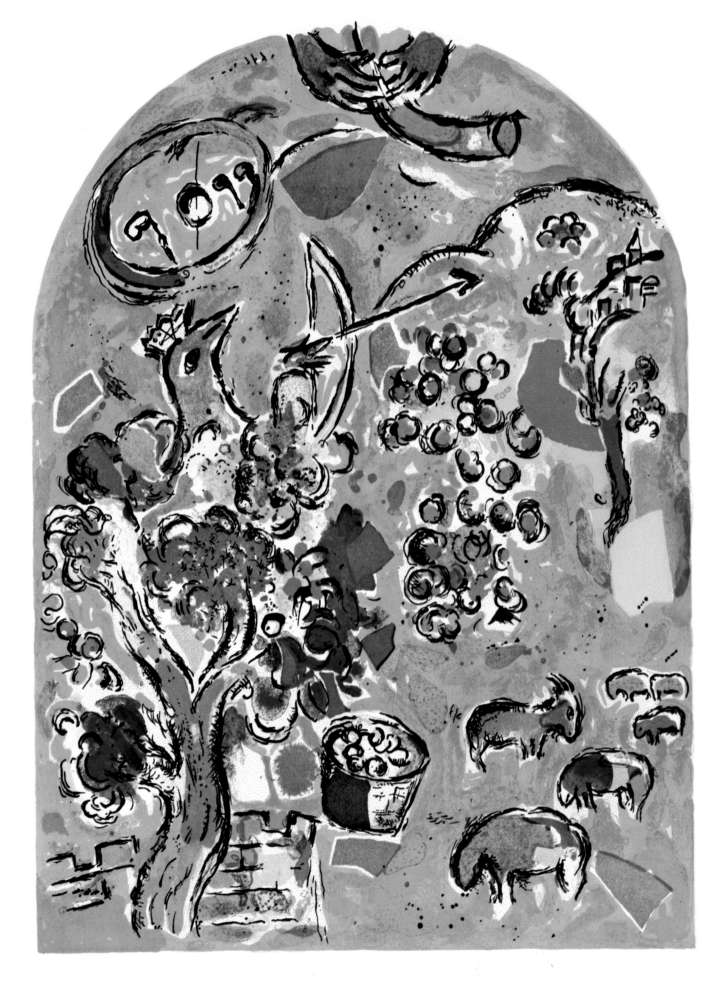

BENJAMIN

Benjamin, whose birth cost the life of his mother Rachel, was the last son of Jacob, who was especially attached to him. His full brother Joseph also loved him very much and proved it to him frequently. The province of Benjamin spread out between that of Ephraim and Judah, as far as the Jordan and the Dead Sea. Famous for the abduction of Shiloh's daughters, the men of Benjamin were proven warriors (Judges 19–21). Within a short time, the tribe gave to Israel a liberator, Ehud the son of Gera, who carried a two-edged sword (Judges 3:15–16), and then its first king, Saul, whom the tribe supported for a long time—even after the coronation of David.

According to the blessing of Jacob:

Benjamin shall ravin as a wolf: in the morning he shall devour the prey, and at night he shall divide the spoil.
GENESIS 49:27

In the lower part of the window rises a superb almost lion-like creature, the animal which symbolizes the tribe. Of violet and carmine, with bloodshot eyes, it stands over its fallen, headless prey, painted with moving tenderness. It is placed against a background of hills and, behind it, gleams—rose and gold, luminous—the Holy City of Jerusalem which was included in Benjamin's territory. Hence the blessing of Moses:

The beloved of the Lord shall dwell in safety by him; and the Lord shall cover him all the day long, and he shall dwell between his shoulders.
DEUTERONOMY 33:12

The shoulders are actually the hills that support the Temple of Jerusalem. The high gate "which was by the house of the Lord" was called the gate of Benjamin (Jeremiah 20:2).

This predominantly blue window, ultramarine and cobalt, is the shining summation of colors and themes of all the windows. The composition is organized with ease and fullness around the imposing central rosette, a gravitation of planets around the sun, a ring of the tribes and human generations under divine light. The circle and the sphere are forms which obsess Chagall. Around the rosette—which has, outside it, a glimpse of fish—the four heraldic animals of the synagogue, symbols of the Jewish faith, reappear (as in the window of Levi). The origin of this last image is the vision of Ezekiel (1:15–21), which associates fabulous animals to the turning of sparkling wheels studded with eyes. Attached to the birds, one also finds the trees of life, with cosmic and mystical significance, which appear in most of the windows. The central panels show, in the heart of the rosette, the splendor of the colors, the suppleness of the leading, the modulation of transitions, and the snowy quality of the whites.

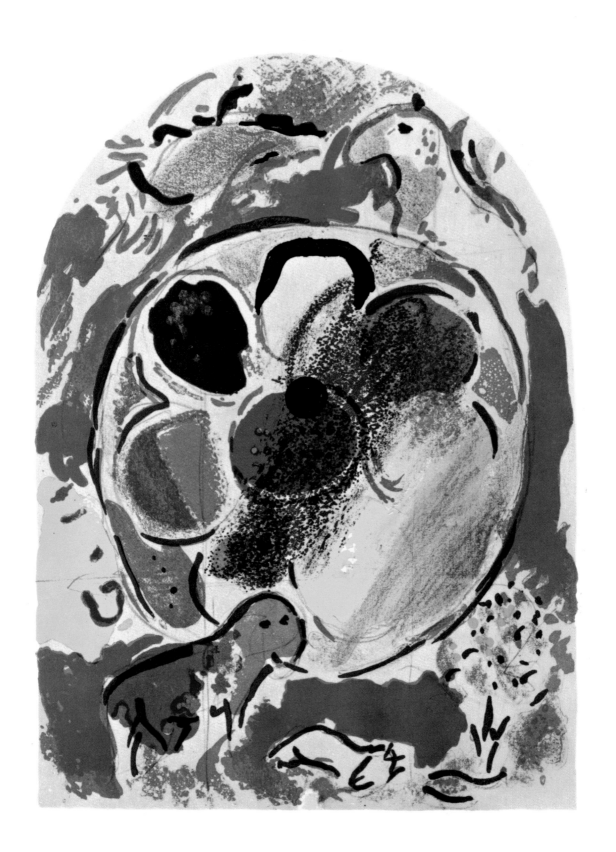

Benjamin shall ravin as a wolf:
in the morning he shall devour the prey,
and at night he shall divide the spoil.

GENESIS 49:27